# HORRID HENRY'S PURPLE HAND GANG
## JOKE BOOK

### Francesca Simon

### Illustrated by Tony Ross

Orion
Children's Books

First published in Great Britain in 2011
by Orion Children's Books
a division of the Orion Publishing Group Ltd
Orion House
5 Upper Saint Martin's Lane
London WC2H 9EA
An Hachette Livre UK Company

Jokes compiled by Sally Byford.

The Orion Publishing Group's policy is to use papers
that are natural, renewable and recyclable products and
made from wood grown in sustainable forests. The logging
and manufacturing processes are expected to conform to
the environmental regulations of the country of origin.

A catalogue record for this book is
available from the British Library.

Printed in Great Britain
by Clays Ltd, St Ives plc

www.horridhenry.co.uk
www.orionbooks.co.uk

# HORRID HENRY'S PURPLE HAND GANG JOKE BOOK

**Francesca Simon** spent her childhood on the beach in California, and then went to Yale and Oxford Universities to study medieval history and literature. She now lives in London with her family. She has written over fifty books and won the Children's Book of the Year in 2008 at the Galaxy British Book Awards for *Horrid Henry and the Abominable Snowman*.

**Tony Ross** is one of Britain's best known illustrators, with many picture books to his name as well as line drawings for many fiction titles. He lives in Oxfordshire.

# CONTENTS

# Hello from Henry

Hey, everyone! I thought my other joke books had the horridest, wickedest, funniest and rudest jokes ever. But who knew my Purple Hand Gang would tell me so many GREAT jokes? Wow! Thanks for doing all the hard work, guys. I think I'll just stomp downstairs and drive Mum and Dad crazy with a few of these zingers. Way to go, gang. The Purple Hand Gang rules!

*Henry*

# MY TOP PURPLE JOKES

*What's purple and fixes pipes?*
A plum-er.

*Why did the elephant paint itself purple?*
So it could hide in the plum tree.

*Why are elephants big and grey?*
If they were small and purple
they'd be grapes.

*What's purple and sounds like an ape?*
A grape.

*What's purple and barks at people?*
A Grape Dane.

*What happens when you drop
a purple rock in
the Red Sea?*
It gets wet.

HENRY: There's a horrible big purple thing on your face!
DAD: Help! What is it?
HENRY: Your nose!

*What's purple, brown and hairy?*
Blackberry jam on toast stuck to the carpet.

*What colour is a burp?*
Burple

# FAVOURITE JOKES FROM MY FANS

*What do you get when you cross a cow and a werewolf?*
A burger that bites back.

*Did you hear about the fight outside the chippie last night?*
Two fish got battered!

*What did Mummy corn say to Baby corn?*
Where's Pop corn?

*Waiter, Waiter, why is there a footprint on my cake?*
Because you said step on it.

*Why didn't the elephant board his plane?*
Because it wasn't a jumbo.

*Which ghost stops goals?*
A ghoulkeeper.

*Which are the three most famous poles?*
North, South and Tad.

*What do you call a daft dinosaur?*
Idiotsaurus.

*Why are bananas so good*
*at gymnastics?*
They are great at doing the splits.

*What's a polygon?*
A dead parrot.

*Where did the spaghetti dance?*
At the meatball.

*What do you call
a lion without
any eyes?*
Lon.

*Doctor, Doctor, I
only have 50
seconds to live.*
Just give me a minute.

*Knock knock.*
Who's there?
*Justin.*
Justin who?
*Justin in time to let me in, toad.*

9

*What do you get when you cross a cat and a parrot?*
A carrot.

*Who is a penguin's favourite aunt?*
Aunt Arctica.

*Why did the boy put sugar on his pillow?*
He wanted to have sweet dreams.

*What do you call a donkey with one eye
and three legs?*
A winky wonky donkey.

*Why are insects clever?*
Because they always know when you're
having a picnic.

*What do you get when
you cross a bomb
and a bad smell?*
A stinkbomb.

*Doctor, Doctor, I can't sleep at night.*
Lie on the edge of your bed and
you'll soon drop off.

*What goes black white
black white black white?*
A penguin rolling down a hill.

*What goes black white
black white black white,
HA HA?*
The penguin that
pushed him.

*Why did the mushroom enjoy the party so much?*
Because he's a fungi.

*What was the magical secret agent called?*
James Wand.

*Did I tell you the joke about butter?*
I'd better not in case you spread it.

*Waiter, Waiter, will my pizza be long?*
No, sir, it'll be round.

*Why are adults always complaining?*
Because they are groan ups.

*Who did Frankenstein
take to the party?*
His ghoulfriend.

*What do you call a scared octopus?*
An octopussy.

*How does a cowboy ride into town on
Friday, stay for three days and ride
out on Friday?*
His horse is called Friday!

*What's an astronaut's favourite
place on the keyboard?*
The spacebar.

*What do hedgehogs
like to eat?*
Prickled onions.

*What do mother penguins tell their
children when they go out?*
Beak careful.

*Why does a cow have a bell?*
Because its horns don't work.

*Why did the cow cross the road?*
To get to the udder side.

*Why did the cow cross the road again?*
It wanted to see a moooooovie.

*What do you call a scared biscuit?*
A cowardy custard cream.

*What do you get when you cross*
*a sheep with a kangaroo?*
A woolly jumper.

*Knock knock.*
Who's there?
*Cash.*
Cash who?
*No thanks, I prefer peanuts.*

*Why did the biscuit*
*go to the doctors?*
Because he felt
crummy.

*What's the difference between roast beef
and pea soup?*
Anyone can roast beef but nobody
can pea soup.

*Why don't leopards cheat in exams?*
They know they'll be spotted.

*What do you call
a man with a seagull
on his head?*
Cliff.

*Waiter, Waiter, there's
a small slug in my salad.*
Sorry, Madam, would you
like a bigger one?

*What do you call a woodpecker with no beak?*
A headbanger.

MISS BATTLE-AXE: Today I want you to write an essay on a goldfish.
RUDE RALPH: I can't do that.
MISS BATTLE-AXE: Why not?
RUDE RALPH: Because I don't have any waterproof ink.

*Why is Europe like a frying pan?*
It has Greece at the bottom.

*Doctor, Doctor, I feel like a cow.*
Sit there and don't moooooove.

*What is a ghost's favourite food?*
Spookhetti.

The three bears came home. Daddy
Bear said, "Who's been eating my
porridge?" and Mummy Bear said,
"Who's been eating my porridge?"
and Baby Bear said, "Never mind
about the porridge, who's nicked
the telly!"

*What do you call*
*a computer superhero?*
A screen saver.

*How do you get a baby astronaut to sleep?*
Rocket.

*Why couldn't the orange run up the hill?*
It ran out of juice.

*Why can't a monster's head be*
*12 inches long?*
Because then it would be a foot.

*Where do wasps go
when they're hurt?*
To the waspital.

*What do you call a sleeping bull?*
A bulldozer.

*A butcher is two metres tall and wears
size thirteen shoes. What does he weigh?*
Meat.

What do you get when you cross
Dr Frankenstein with a pig?
Frankenswine.

What do computers eat?
Microchips.

What do you call a lion with toothache?
Rory.

What does an octopus wear when it's cold?
A coat of arms.

*Where do you catch a flying pig?*
At the airpork.

*What do you call a fish with no eye?*
A fsh.

MISS BATTLE-AXE: Name the
four seasons.
GREEDY GRAHAM: Salt, pepper,
mustard and vinegar.

*What's the cleverest
species of dinosaur?*
A Thesaurus.

*Who shouted knickers at the big bad wolf?*
Little rude riding hood.

*Why did the boy carry a clock*
*and a bird on Halloween?*
For tick or tweet.

*Knock knock.*
Who's there?
*Bacon.*
Bacon who?
*Bacon a cake for your birthday.*

*What do you get when you cross*
*a computer with an elephant?*
Lots of memory.

*What did the frog order at the fast*
*food restaurant?*
French flies and a diet croak.

*What goes up the stairs*
*but never moves?*
A carpet.

*How do you make a fruit punch?*
Give it boxing lessons.

*What do you call a man with a map on his head?*
Miles.

*Who gives presents to children, then gobbles them up?*
Santa Jaws.

*How do snails keep their shells so shiny?*
They use snail varnish.

*What do witches
put on their hair?*
Scare spray.

*Which painting is never happy?*
The Moaning Lisa.

*What are the werewolves' cousins called?*
The whywolf, the whatwolf and the
whenwolf.

*Can I tell you a joke about a wall?*
Yes please.
*No, because you'll never get over it.*

A man came round to our house asking for donations for the local swimming pool. I gave him a glass of water!

*What does a ghost call his mum and dad?*
Transparents.

*What's the Earth's favourite bit of a pizza?*
The crust.

*What do cows eat for breakfast?*
MOOOuesli.

*Which two letters are bad for your teeth?*
DK.

*What does a dentist do on a rollercoaster?*
He braces himself.

*What did the elf use to make himself taller?*
Elf raising flour.

*Why was the skeleton afraid of the dog?*
Because dogs like bones!

*What do you get when you cross
a pig and a woodchopper?*
Pork chops.

*What do you call James Bond in the bath?*
Bubble O Seven.

*What do you call a
woman with two
toilets on her head?*
Lulu.

DAD: I hope you're
not talking in class
any more.
HORRID HENRY: I'm not talking
any more, I'm talking the same amount.

*I saw Esau sitting on a see-saw.
How many s's in that?*
There aren't any s's in THAT!

*Doctor, Doctor, I've got a strawberry growing
on my head.*
Well, put some cream on it.

*What runs but has no legs?*
Water.

*Waiter, Waiter, do
you serve fish?*
Sit down, Sir,
we serve anyone.

*What did the plumber say to his wife
when their marriage ended?*
It's over flow.

*What's the sweetest
insect?*
    A humbug.

*Knock knock.*
Who's there?
*Egbert.*
Egbert who?
*Egbert no bacon.*

*What do you call
a rooster that
wakes you up at
the same time
every morning?*
An alarm cluck.

*What do you
call a skeleton
snake?*
A rattler.

*What's the difference between an African
elephant and an Indian elephant?*
About 6,000 kilometres.

MUM: Shall I put the kettle on?
DAD: No, I prefer the dress you're
wearing now.

LADY: Can I try that dress on
in the window?
SHOPKEEPER: No way, try it
on in the changing room.

*Doctor, Doctor, I think I'm shrinking.*
Well, you'll have to be a little patient.

*What happened to the cat that
ate a ball of wool?*
She had mittens.

*What has 22 legs, 11 heads and 2 wings?*
A football team.

*A bee just stung me on my arm.*
Which one?
*I don't know, they all look the same to me.*

*Why did the sheep cross the road?*
It wanted to go to the baaaarbers.

*What do you call a bee that lives in a graveyard?*
A zom-bee.

*What cheese is made backwards?*
Edam.

*Doctor, Doctor, I keep thinking I'm a canary.*
Perch yourself down and I'll tweet you in
a minute.

*What did the ghost teacher say to
her pupils?*
Look at the board – I'm going
to go through it again.

*What do you get when you dial
34027358923759235872935873589857?*
A sore finger.

*Why do hens watch TV?*
For hentertainment.

*Why is my brother built upside down?*
Because his nose runs and his feet smell.

*What did one volcano say to the other volcano?*
Do you lava me like I lava you?

*What do you get when you cross a cow,
a sheep and a baby goat?*
The Milky Baa kid.

*Why did the submarine go red?*
Because it saw the ship's bottom.

*What did the parrot take for his headache?*
Parrotcetemol.

*A horse went up to two cows and said,*
*"Excuse me, where are the toilets?"*
"That's amazing," said one cow to the
other, "a horse that can speak."

*What do you call a man*
*with a tree growing out*
*of his head?*
Edward.

*Why did a man with*
*one hand cross the road?*
To get to the second
hand shop.

One day a man was walking down the street with a penguin. A policeman saw them and told the man to take the penguin to the zoo. The next day the policeman saw the man again with the penguin, and said, "I thought I told you to take the penguin to the zoo." The man said, "I did, and we had such fun that I'm taking him to the cinema today."

*What's black when you buy it, red when you use it and grey when you throw it away?*
Coal.

*What's a sheep's favourite snack?*
Chocolate baaaaaars.

*There were three cookies in the jar last night and now there's only one. What's your excuse?*
It was dark so I must have missed it!

*What do you call a man who likes fishing?*
Rod.

*What did the chick say when his mum laid an orange?*
Look what marmalade.

*What does an alien from Mars like to eat?*
Martian-mallows.

*Why do zebras like old movies?*
Because they are black and white.

*What happened to the wooden car with the wooden wheels and the wooden engine?*
It wooden go.

*What did the teacher say when the horse walked into the classroom?*
Why the long face?

*What are a monster's favourite fairground rides?*
The helter skeleton and the roller ghoster.

*How does a dog stop the DVD player?*
He presses the paws button.

A guest in a posh hotel says to the waiter, "Can I order two boiled eggs, one undercooked and runny and one overcooked and tough, with some rubbery bacon and burnt toast."

The waiter said, "Sir, we can't serve such a dreadful breakfast!"

"Why not?" the guest replied. "That's what I got here yesterday!"

*Knock knock.*
Who's there?
*A dare.*
A dare who?
*A dare once, but I'm bald now.*

*Why do dogs run round in circles?*
It's hard to run in squares.

*What do you call a skunk that's disappeared?*
Ex-stinked.

*What has a bed but never sleeps?*
A river.

*Why did the bald man stick his head
out of the window?*
To get some fresh hair.

*Which travels faster – heat or cold?*
Heat, because you can catch a cold.

*How do you make a jacket last?*
Make the trousers first.

*Why is history like a fruitcake?*
It's full of dates.

*What did the scarf say to the hat?*
You go on ahead and I'll hang around.

*What comes once in a minute, twice in a moment, but never in a thousand years?*
The letter M.

*What smells worse than a skunk?*
Two skunks.

*Did you hear about the wolves'*
*all-night party?*
It was a howling success.

*When do birds celebrate their dads?*
On feather's day.

*What do you call an animal that*
*talks too much?*
A yak.

*Why did Santa have to close his factory?*
For elf and safety.

*What do you get when you cross a cow
and an earthquake?*
A milkshake.

*Why don't oysters share?*
Because they're shellfish.

*What do you call a parrot with no wings?*
A walkie talkie.

*How do you catch a rabbit?*
Hide behind a tree and
make a noise like a carrot.

*What can you serve but can't eat?*
Tennis balls.

*What did the lion say when he saw two men in a car?*
Yum, yum, meals on wheels.

*Why did the robber take a bath?*
He wanted to make a clean getaway.

*Why did the overweight man throw his wallet in the bin?*
He wanted to lose a couple of pounds.

Which vehicle is the same going
backwards or forwards?
Racecar.

What's the best place for a mouse
to leave its boat?
The hickory dickory dock.

Why was the broom late for breakfast?
It overswept.

*How can you swallow a plug?*
Gulp backwards.

*What goes 'oom oom'?*
A cow walking
backwards.

*What did the snake say when it was*
*offered a piece of cheese?*
Thanks, I'll just have a slither.

*What gets bigger the more you take away*
*from it?*
A hole.

*I went to the optician's to collect my*
*glasses and guess who I bumped into?*
Everyone!

*What's the difference between a nail
and a boxer?*
One gets knocked in and one
gets knocked out.

*Knock knock.*
Who's there?
*Scott.*
Scott who?
*Scott nothing to do with you.*

*Why did the Mexican throw his wife off the cliff?*
Tequila!

*What did the rabbit say to the carrot?*
It was nice gnawing you.

*What do you get when you cross a chicken with a cement mixer?*
A bricklayer.

*Waiter, Waiter, I can't eat this soup.*
*Call the manager.*
It's no use, Madam. He won't eat it either.

*Doctor, Doctor, I've broken my arm in two places.*
Well, don't go there again.

*My dog has no nose.*
Really, how does he smell?
*Terrible!*

*What kind of tree has hands?*
A palm tree.

*Why are hairdressers such good drivers?*
They know all the short cuts.

*What do you call a woman*
*with a sheep on her head?*
Baa–baa–ra.

*Why is a sofa like
a roast turkey?*
Because it's full
of stuffing.

*Why did the tuna go to Hollywood?*
She wanted to be a starfish.

*Why was the baby ant confused?*
Because all his uncles were ants.

*What has six legs but only uses four?*
A man on a horse.

*What's the tallest building?*
A library because it has so many stories.

*What do you call a pig with no clothes on?*
Streaky bacon.

*What happened when two fat men were in a race?*
One ran in short bursts and the other ran in burst shorts.

*Why did your brother wear a wet t-shirt all day?*
The label said wash and wear.

*What's white and yellow and travels
at 160 mph?*
A train driver's egg sandwich.

*Why do some people like eating snails?*
Because they don't like fast food.

PIANIST: Do you think I have
a gift for playing?
DAD: No, but I'll give you
a gift for stopping.

*What do you call a man who forgets to put his pants on?*
Nicholas.

*How do you know that carrots are good for your eyesight?*
Have you ever seen a rabbit wearing glasses?

*Did you hear about the man on a seafood diet?*
If he saw food, he ate it.

*Why is school like a shower?*
One wrong turn and you're in hot water.

*What begins with a P and ends with
an E and has a million letters in it?*
A Post Office.

*What kind of crisps can fly?*
Plane.

*What do you call a sleeping dinosaur?*
A dinosnore.

*Knock knock.*
Who's there?
*Justin.*
Justin who?
*Justin in time for school, ha ha.*

*What happens to a cat if it eats a lemon?*
It turns into a sourpuss.

*Why did Horrid Henry take an empty doughnut to the dentist?*
He wanted to get a filling.

*Why is the letter T like an island?*
Because it's in the middle of water.

*Why does a seagull live near the sea?*
If it lived near the bay, it'd be a bagel.

*What song did they play when the baker got married?*
Here crumbs the bride.

*What do you call a boy with a spade
on his head?*
Doug.

*What do you call a boy without a spade
on his head?*
Douglas.

*How do you make an octopus laugh?*
Ten tickles.

*Which bird succeeds?*
A budgie without any teeth.

*What's a pelican's favourite dish?*
Anything that fits the bill.

*What did the little bird say to the big bird?*
Peck on someone your own size.

*What do you call a man who likes doing exercise?*
Jim.

*What's always coming, but never arrives?*
Tomorrow.

*How did the baker get an electric shock?*
He stood on a bun and a current ran up his leg.

Who gets the
sack as soon as
he starts work?
A postman.

What goes, "Quick-quick!"?
A duck with the hiccups.

What do you call a clumsy bee?
A tumble bee.

Why did the
girl throw the
butter out of
the window?
To see a
butter fly.

*Why couldn't the chicken find her eggs?*
She mislaid them.

*When's the best time
to buy a bird?*
When it's going
"cheep cheep".

*What happens if you call 666?*
You get an upside-down policeman.

*What do you call a man with
a paper bag on his head?*
Russell.

*Why did Singing Soraya
climb the ladder?*
To reach the high
notes.

*Why did the boy
climb the ladder?*
He wanted to get to
high school.

*Why is your pet
always smiling?*
Because it's a
grinny pig.

*What do you call a man with a truck on his
head?*
Laurie.

*What's worse than an elephant with
a sore trunk?*
A centipede with sore feet.

*Why can't you tell
Humpty Dumpty
a joke?*
Because he'll crack up.

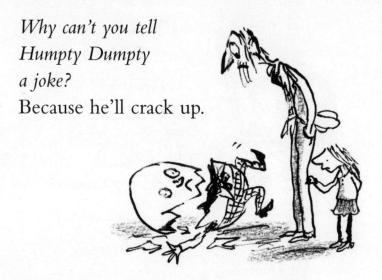

*What did one wall say to the other wall?*
Meet you at the corner.

*Waiter, Waiter, what do you call this?*
It's bean soup, sir.
*I don't care what it's been —
what is it now?*

*Why did the chicken cross the road?*
To get to the shop.
*Did you find that funny? Well, neither did
the chicken because the shop was closed.*

*Why did the girl study on the aeroplane?*
She wanted a higher education

*Why couldn't the pirate play cards?*
Because he was standing on the deck.

*What do you call a piece of wood with nothing to do?*
Bored.

*Doctor, Doctor, I feel like a racehorse.*
Take one of these every four laps.

*Why did the banana go to the doctor?*
He wasn't peeling well.

*What do you call two robbers?*
A pair of knickers.

*What do you call an eight-legged cat?*
An octopussy..

*Why was the computer so cold?*
Because its windows were open.

*How did the bubblegum cross the road?*
It was stuck to the chicken's foot.

*What do you call a quiet bee?*
A mumble bee.

# EVEN MORE PURPLE JOKES

PETER: Henry, look, my tongue's gone purple.

HENRY: **Bleccch! Go and stick it out at Margaret.**

PETER: Will that help?

HENRY: **No, but I don't like Margaret.**

*What's purple and leaps from a tree?*
A squirrel.
*Why is it purple?*
Because it choked on a nut.

*What colour do you get when*
*you pull a burp?*
Burp-pull.

*What's purple and rides a horse?*
Alexander the Grape.

MARGARET: Knock Knock.
SUSAN: Who's there?
MARGARET: The purple.
SUSAN: The purple who?
MARGARET: The purple who
   live next door.

*What's purple with a hundred hairy legs?*
I don't know, but there's one running
up your leg.

*What's a cat's favourite colour?*
Purrrrrrr-ple.

*What's big, purple and ugly?*
You!

*What do you call a purple dinosaur
with a banana in each ear?*
Anything you like –
he can't hear you.

HORRID HENRY: **What rhymes with red?**

LAZY LINDA: Bed.

HORRID HENRY: **What rhymes with green?**

PERFECT PETER: Bean

HORRID HENRY: **What rhymes with blue?**

RUDE RALPH: Boo!

HORRID HENRY: **What rhymes with purple?**

BEEFY BERT: I dunno.

**Do you?**

**Horrid Henry** would like to thank all the Purple Hand Gang members who sent in their totally brilliant, utterly wicked jokes.

| | |
|---|---|
| *Mia, Leicester* | *Raahul, Harrow* |
| *George, London* | *Katie, Liverpool* |
| *Jordan, Scarborough* | *Mileena, Ipswich* |
| *Olivia, Rotherham* | *Kapitalina, Antwerp* |
| *Cristina, Liverpool* | *Caitlin, Dunedin* |
| *Matt, Eastleigh* | *Ollie, Perthshire* |
| *Nadine, UK* | *David, Glasgow* |
| *Murtaza, Sharjah* | *Alex, Scunthorpe* |
| *Izzy, Wigan* | *Jodie, UK* |

Lily, UK

Gemma, Birmingham

Megan, South Woodham

Bilal Ahmed, Halifax

Abigail, England

Shyla, India

Kayaiya, London

Max, Gatley

Aminath, UK

Saaraj, Preston

Lauren, Hampshire

Jack, Doncaster

Phillipa, Coventry

Mitchell, London

Rebekah, Shropshire

Charlotte, Birmingham

Maisie, Rugby

Lois, Preston

Imogine, Manchester

Shauna, Nottingham

Jasmin, Leeds

Farwah, Luton

Rohail, London

Cameron, Lincolnshire

Alysha, England

Ari, UK

Ellie, UK

Rahul, England

Chantel, Norwich

Calum, Manchester

Emma, New Milton

Dana, Barwell

Kirsten, Greystone

Kelly, London

Beth, Lancaster

Messy, London

Maria, England

Chazii, Cambridge

Faye, Enfield

Alex, Slough

Sally, Trowbridge

Sahar, London

Bethany, England

Rico, London

Shane-Deon, London    Bethany, Matlock
Rebecca, Truro    Suneet, Dublin
Lauren, Leeds    Kimran, Birmingham
Rachel, St Helens    Amana, London
Megan, Romford    Kayleigh, Ireland
Jasmine, Shropshire    Bethany, London
Megan, Manchester    Leah, Bradford
Eleanor, Chorley    Jennifer, Northampton
Ryan, Kincardine    Courtney, Andover
Ben, Wigan    Jessica, Warrington
Holly, UK    Ben, London
Benjamin, Leicester    Megan, Bury
Sannah, Birmingham    Louise,
Liam, London     Stoke on Trent
Libby, Coventry    Britney, UK
David, Flintshir    Emma, Liverpool
Tiegan, UK    Francesca, Dubai
Evie, Epsom    Rebekah, UK
Alfie, Essex    Kirsten, Glasgow
Kerry, Coventry    Aimee, Leeds
Robbie, Sedbergh    Holly, Blackburn
Ben, Milverton    Ellie, Liverpool
Hannah, Blackburn    Yasmine, Cowley

Ellie, Yorkshire

Miriam, Gloucester

Jasmine, Aylesbury

Bradley, UK

Lucy, Oldham

Talha, Manchester

Orla, England

Bobbi, Liverpool

Shea, Armagh

Leah, Manchester

Chloe, UK

Emma, England

Ellie, Wirral

Ellie, Littleborough

Danielle, Basingstoke

Mia, London

Lauren, Liverpool

Dominic, Ellesmere Port

Everette, Baltimore

Madeline, Leeds

Caitlin, Dublin

Roshni, London

Craig, Bishops Stortford

Lucia, London

Libby, Bolton

Cara, Norwich

Luca, Brighton & Hove

Joe, Derby

Mia, Manchester

Alisha, Mexico City

Kaisha, England

Joshua, Swindon

Sammy, UK

Susiksha, England

Ben, Hull

Lucy, UK

Jasmin, Wolverhampton

Sam, Bradford

Ahsan, London

Jay, South Ockendon

Lewis, London

Holly, Chatham

Jack, London

Morgan, Scotland

Mark, Leicester

Tammy, Sheffield

Jade, Hastings

Leah, London

Ben, Taunton

Rebecca, Harrogate

Callum, Tividale

Yusuf, London

James, Lisbon

Zoe, Birmingham

Sarah, Nottingham

Jacob, Liverpool

Ellis, Malvern

Samuel, Ajman

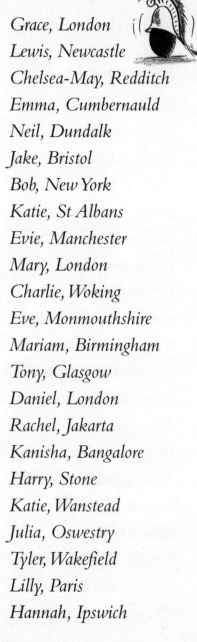

Lauren, Dollingstown

Teesta, Mumbai

Zoya, Manchester

Maryam, London

Saheem, Northampton

Caitlin, Durham

Caleb, Chongqing

Jess, Swanwick

Marie, Hampshire

Mairi, Stirling

Grace, London

Lewis, Newcastle

Chelsea-May, Redditch

Emma, Cumbernauld

Neil, Dundalk

Jake, Bristol

Bob, New York

Katie, St Albans

Evie, Manchester

Mary, London

Charlie, Woking

Eve, Monmouthshire

Mariam, Birmingham

Tony, Glasgow

Daniel, London

Rachel, Jakarta

Kanisha, Bangalore

Harry, Stone

Katie, Wanstead

Julia, Oswestry

Tyler, Wakefield

Lilly, Paris

Hannah, Ipswich

Irandip, Wolverhampton

Henna, Oldham

Thomas, UK

Amal, Birmingham

Lillee, Plymouth

Haroon, Birmingham

Hassan, Dublin

Lucas, Guernsey

Ned, Purley

Teeba, London

Mhairi, Torphins

Paige, Newark

Erin, Barrhead

Lucia, Margate

Toby, Congleton

Alessio, London

Mia, Kent

Alice, Swadlincote

Anant, Mumbai

Kamilla, Stourport

Harrison, Manchester

Christopher, UK

Alex, Essex

Rebecca, Middlesbrough

Joel, Peterhead

Kirsty, Belfast

Elizabeth, London

Jasmine, Portsmouth

Lydia, Cleveland

Alice, England

Shannon, Tadworth

Nikita, Torrington

Joshua, Essex

Ashleigh, Oldham

Isabel, Exeter

Adam, Douglas

Pearse, Dublin

Jessica, Liverpool

Presley, Manchester

Brandon, Crewe

Dylan, Shrewsbury

Lucy, Chatham

Ellie, Mistley

Charlotte, Farnham

Jake, Dublin

Shania, Solihull

Nathan, Preston

Rihanna, London

Sabbir, London

Shreyas, Milton Keynes

Emily, Dublin

Rhianna, Oxford

Jane, London

Emily, London

Joey, London

James, Leeds

Talia, Oldham

Alisha, Birmingham

Darcy, Durham

Hafsa, Manchester

Bláthnaid, Carrickmore

Vikram, Newcastle

Nina, UK

Megan, London

Hashim, London

Charlie, Bristol

Adam, London

Britney, Newcastle

Finn, Middlesbrough

Patrick, Belfast

Catherine, Liverpool

Louise, Pontypridd

Salom, Luton

Jake, Manchester

Kelsey, Retford

Niamh, Highwycombe

Gabriella, Durban

Lily, Cape Town

Georgia, Hull

Charlotte, London

Zaynab, Birmingham

Colm, Kerry

Antara, Kolkata

Thea, Chichester

Matthew, Walsall

Faith, Kent

Linards, Ireland

Liberty, Haringey

Kiera, Leamington

Aidan, Manchester

Ben, Sutton

Susanna, London

Conor, Dunbar

Luke, Cork

Ewan, UK

Sana, Al Ain

Georgia, Reigate

Louie, Reading

Sara, London

Clio, Newtown

Michelle, London

Abinaya, Stevenage

Josie, London

Lauren, UK

Callum, Paisley

Eli, Wales

Nicole, Dundrod

Teuta, Harrow

Jessica, Bedford

Afiq, Singapore

Tamsin, Thanet

Bobbie, Grimsby

Megan, Wolverhampton

Sharna, Westcliff

Tyler,
    Paddock Wood

Jodie, Shropshire

Shah, London

Gemma, Johannesburg

Brittany, Victoria

Shaye, London

Maya, Tipton

Sian, Plymouth

Holly, Lancaster

Dhruv, Chennai

Rosie, Coventry

Toby, Derby

Camila, London

Jessica, Eastbourne

Chloe, Kirkby

Liam, Carlisle

Jed, Newcastle

Esha, Rochdale

Alfie, Coventry

Yasmin, Manchester

Isabelle, Scotland

Jessica, Nottingham

Sophie, Saltash          Maxine, Surrey

Jolene, Belfast          Paul, Liverpool

Kyra, UK                 Eleanor, Benfleet

Jack, Dagenham           Luke, Oldham

Mohammed, Qatar          Nerissa, Eastbourne

Hannah, Dunfermline      Mayyah, Northampton

Aishwarya, Lusaka        Tegan, UK

Oliver, Croydon          Evie, Leicestershire

Saz, New York            Emily, Leipzig

Anzum, London            Jude, Richmond

Abi, Newcastle           Harrison, Brereton

GuanMin, Singapore       Monet, London

Jackie, London           Sian, Tamworth

Cassy, Liverpool         Adrienne, Northampton

Zara, Birmingham         Hannah, Newport

Katie, Oswestry          Sajeevan, London

Samuel, Andover          Grace, West Midlands

Stephanie, Newbury       Ella, Waltham Cross

Olivia, UK               Jaya, Orpington

Gemma, Luton             Gemma, UK

Kieran, UK               Jade, Lydd

Jada, London             Liberty, Portsmouth

Phil, Liverpool          Megan, Wales

Emily, Bridgend

Moo, USA

Donna, England

Clio, Powys

Jasmine, Rugby

Michael, Lochgilphead

Alexia, Wimbledon

Leela, Broadstairs

Thomas, Tapei City

Rory, Shipley

Chloe, England

Samantha, Caterham

Kirstin, Watford

Shazna, Woking

Amy, Shrewsbury

Ceri, Forfar

Leilla, Surbiton

Owen, Harwich

Sophie, Nottinghamshire

Evie, Grimsby

Olivia, Plymouth

Jaya, West Yorkshire

Adil, Preston

Caitlin, Kilsyth

Nicole, Billericay

Lauren, England

Liberty, Nottingham

Chantelle, York

Shanaj, London

Anya, Northampton

Max, London

Oliver, Sidcup

Maebh, Co. Cork

Libby, Manchester

Jodi, Glasgow

Millie, Guernsey

Joshua, Walsall

Morgan, Glasgow

Jadene, Helston

William, Tunbridge Wells

Deana, Newark

Chloe, Nottingham

Luke, Derby

Benjamin, Studham

Jake, Leeds

Stephen, Rushall

Millie, Rugby                 Lauren, Southend on Sea

Marie, Rushall                Gemma, Falkirk

Josh, Basildon                Courtney, Sunderland

Lia, Blackpool                Priya, Birmingham

Jonathan, Ipswich             Connor, Burntisland

Zac, Brighton                 Georgia, Marton

Celie, London                 Yagoda, London

Georgia, England              Tracey, Airdrie

Ivan, East Kilbride           Isaac, Nottingham

Jaz, Kent                     Megan, Whitely

Kelsey, London                Nasar, Burton

Claudia, Cirencester          Tom, London

Reilly, Derbyshire            Abigail, Peterborough

Kirandeep, Coventry           Amber, Hartlepool

Elysia, UK                    Annabelle, Wilmslow

Liam, Norwich                 Elliot, Taunton

Aaqib, Bradford               Charley, Nottingham

Ellie, Darlington             Raeece, Manchester

Katie, Roscommon              Zain, Manchester

Lily, Rushden                 Keita, Preston

Sandhya, England              Georgia, Blackpool

Kishan, London                Cariad, Essex

Lauren, Dunstable             Zhanae, Nottingham

Myles, Manchester

Devon, Egham

Elana, Scotland

Mollie, Manchester

Ethan, Nottingham

Musab, Manchester

Ella, Swansea

Maryam, Didcot

Callum, Kirkcudbright

Kitty, Coventry

Rebecca, London

Finley, Lee on the Solent

India, Clevedon

Joe, Stoke

Bobbie-May,
Kingstanding

Sam, Belfast

Ella, Leicestershire

Emily, Hockley

Toni, Lincoln

Susie, London

Krishma, Staffs

Farhan, London

Louise,
    Great Wyrley

Madina, England

Manoli, London

Melvin, London

Marsha, Ascot

Fenton, Hoghton

Georgia, London

Courtney, Liverpool

Clara, Chichester

Megan, Spalding

Leanne, Glasgow

Richard, Longford

Georgia, Sheffield

Ali, Harlow

Zachary,
    Nantwich

Jake,
    Wolverhampton

Morgan, Barnsley

Jack, UK

Evie, Willenhall

Ryan Manchester

# More HORRID HENRY

*Horrid Henry*

*Horrid Henry and the Secret Club*

*Horrid Henry Tricks the Tooth Fairy*

*Horrid Henry's Nits*

*Horrid Henry Gets Rich Quick*

*Horrid Henry's Haunted House*

*Horrid Henry and the Mummy's Curse*

*Horrid Henry's Revenge*

*Horrid Henry and the Bogey Babysitter*

*Horrid Henry's Stinkbomb*

*Horrid Henry's Underpants*

*Horrid Henry Meets the Queen*

*Horrid Henry and the Mega-Mean Time Machine*

*Horrid Henry and the Football Fiend*

*Horrid Henry's Christmas Cracker*

*Horrid Henry and the Abominable Snowman*

*Horrid Henry Robs the Bank*

*Horrid Henry Wakes the Dead*

*Horrid Henry Rocks*

For a complete list of **HORRID HENRY** titles,
visit **www.horridhenry.co.uk**